Testimonials

Jay has succeeded in shedding a refreshing light on how to extract your stories and transform them to the written form. Through his own stories and natural humor, Jay makes the journey simple, fun, and above all, possible!
Patty Kreamer - Kreamer Connect, Inc.
Author, The Power of Simplicity

Trust me...the book you are holding is a gem. I could not put it down. Jay takes you by the hand and leads you down a road of personal discovery as he encourages you to write your own true story.
Eleanor Schano
TV Broadcast Journalist
Host - "LifeQuest"
WQED Multimedia

Jay breaks up the monumental process of memoir writing into easy-to-understand steps. Follow them diligently, and you'll be well on your way to creating a lasting legacy for generations to come.
Jill Cueni-Cohen, journalist

The Stories of our Days is a reader-friendly book, particularly useful for beginning and experienced writers. Light humor and a variety of anecdotes and examples make for an interesting learning experience.
Don DiMarco
Retired Educator/ Author, Flaggadoo's Alley

Beginning the writing process with Jay is like enrolling in a humor seminar and group therapy at the same time. Buckle your seatbelt and prepare for the ride.
Nancy Mramor, Ph.D.
Author, Spiritual Fitness

The Stories of Our Days

EXPANDED JOURNAL EDITION

The Stories of Our Days

Writing Your True Story
Using Techniques of Fiction

by

Jay Speyerer

Legacy Road Communications
Pittsburgh, Pennsylvania

ISBN: 0-9764729-2-9
Expanded Journal Edition

Published by: Legacy Road Communications
PO Box 7976
Pittsburgh, PA 15216
www.legacyroad.net

This book was printed in the United States of America.

Dedication

For the absent storytellers:
William and Lora Speyerer
Sara Ortelt
You got me started

My daughter, Emma
You keep me going

Contents

Acknowledgments

A book might be written by one person, but no book is truly written alone. My thanks to: Bea Briske and Jeff for historical fact-checking; Jill Cueni-Cohen, Mary Cvetan, Don DiMarco, Twila Green, and Patty Kreamer for expert reader's insights; Donna Herrle of Drawing Conclusions for the cover design; Dr. Nancy Mramor and Rebecca Suhoza for psychological perspectives; and Hank Walshak for reader insights and a line edit that went above and beyond the call of friendship.

Author's Note

This is an interactive book. That means that you participate. The chapters of the book comprise what I know about story telling; the journal/note pages that follow the chapters are for you to complete. Use them as a journal. Use them for notes. But please ... use them.

Remember...

You might be very interesting today,
but you'll be fascinating in fifty years.

Preface
You can do this

You can write your *true* stories using techniques of *fiction writing*. That's because, deep down, you understand story.

As a species, we have been using language as we know it for about 30,000 years. The Cro-Magnons (*homo sapiens sapiens*) were the first to employ sophisticated grammar and syntax, not the grunts and hand signals of our earlier ancestors (not that there's anything wrong with that). Cro-Magnon society was primitive, yet the people were skilled at making both tools and fitted clothing. Odds are, at the end of a hard day's hunting by The Man and gathering by The Woman, stories flew across the cookfire. The Man told of the wooly mammoth that got away, and The Woman rolled her eyes. Then The Man got wise and went out and told the story to the other men, who actually appreciated it.

(By the way, Cro-Magnons were essentially us. Give one of them relaxed fit jeans, a Hard Rock Café t-shirt, and a riding lawn mower and you couldn't distinguish him from your average suburbanite.)

Our hunter might have used some of the same techniques we use today in recounting our exploits to our friends during happy hour or at the chamber of commerce luncheon: providing visual details; using broad gestures and facial expressions; maybe even employing a bit of exaggeration.

This storytelling art has been handed down over the millennia. Before the coming of writing roughly 6,000 years ago, the creation of artworks and the oral recounting of events were the only ways to pass history on to the next generation. When societies changed from being nomadic hunter-gatherers to agrarian village dwellers, the cultures became more complicated. Writing was essential for keeping track of such societal elements as property boundaries, conquered lands, and religions. Good thing someone in the Middle East came up with the first alphabet.

When I say "fiction techniques," I'm not suggesting that you make things up. You simply put into print what good oral storytellers do vocally: provide description of details, employ dialogue, generate suspense, and dole out information logically and gradually.

Your stories should not *look* like fiction; you'll simply be using fiction-writing techniques, and sparely at that. Not too much dialogue, minimal atmosphere, and certainly no artificially constructed plot. This is reality you're writing about; you're telling us how the events unfolded. But with these techniques, your readers will be able to paint a clearer picture in their minds. Therein lies the true art of storytelling.

Because fiction is close to my heart (I've read and written a lot of it), I'll be returning to that idea of painting pictures in your readers' minds. Mental movies, if you will.

We'll touch on some of the major concepts of writing, such as structure, point of view, description, and dialogue, as well as the writing process itself. And as a bonus, you'll even learn what rules of grammar you can ignore!

You say you're not a writer? That's either because you haven't written anything yet or you haven't tried this technique. If you can use language, you can write. It might take more work and practice for some people than for others, but if you can read this, you can write your story.

What makes writing more challenging is the fact that the stories are yours. Telling someone else's story would involve little or no emotional investment by you. But telling your own story, with all its stratified emotions — some deep, some shallow — opens up all sorts of psychic sinkholes. You can easily dwell on the emotions of an event and take forever to write about it. Writing about an event in your life will eventually help you sort out how you feel about it, but the process probably won't be quick – not if you haven't come to terms with the emotional context.

Whether it's Beowulf or The Big Chill, we are so conditioned to storytelling that we know on a deep, unspoken level when a story works and when it doesn't. We might not be able to say what's wrong technically – too long a setup, poor character development, stilted dialogue – but we do know that a problem exists. That's because stories are so much a part of us that I'm convinced they're encoded in our DNA. With a bit of help, such as this book, you can tell a story to enthrall.

If a Cro-Magnon could do it, you can.

Introduction
"The Banana and the Muse"

I have a love/hate relationship with bananas. And with writing. Bananas first.

I like bananas. They taste good, they're good for you, and they're a good source of potassium to regulate your heart. Each one comes with its own wrapper. Buy them green if you like, then wait for them to turn yellow. But sometimes you wait too long to eat them and the freckles take over. Actually those freckles are called sugar spots, and FYI, bananas are perfectly good to eat even if they do have a few freckles. But sometimes, they get a lot of freckles, and those freckles even begin to merge, and then the bananas get that funny, strong taste. When that happens, you don't slice them onto your corn flakes — you make banana bread.

What is this, you're asking, *The Joy of Cooking*? Why is he telling us all this? For one thing, I'm constructing an analogy, a favored device of writers (chapter two). It's also because some things are simply out of our control and bananas are one of those things. Bananas have their own process: green to yellow to yellow-with-freckles to brown. (We won't discuss the black stage; you might be eating.) Sometimes they go straight from green to brown; that's like skipping steps in the writing process. Bananas serve to point out this writer's confessed issues with procrastination and control: I want the banana to be ready to eat when I want to eat it. But a banana has its own agenda. So does the writing muse.

In a perfect universe, I could sit down at the keyboard whenever I had a block of time at my disposal and simply write. After all, I have the opportunity, the proper environment for writing (which varies with the personality of the writer, see chapter nine), and a lot of life left in my laptop battery or a table next to an electrical outlet. *She* is the only ingredient that is lacking.

She appears without warning, this muse of ours. I'm not being sexist in using the feminine pronoun, as the Greek muses were indeed regarded as being female. Their names were Calliope, Clio, Erato, Euterpe, Melpomene, Polyhymnia, Terpsichore, Thalia, and Urania, alphabetically speaking. Four of the muses were concerned with various areas of writing – Calliope with epic poetry, Erato with love poetry, Melpomene with tragedy, and Thalia with comedy – so we have no one particular name to use in conjuring up an inspirational figure. For our purposes, she will remain The Muse.

What follows are the psychological explanations for The Muse, but these explanations should not displace the magic of writing. Knowing the how of a thing does not diminish the wonder of it. (This book is G-rated, so please furnish your own example.)

The 5-Step Program

Insight: Let It Be.

Insight can come from a great variety of sources. You might witness an event — some act of unusual kindness or cruelty or plain and simple oddness — that exemplifies the other humans with whom you share the planet.

You might write about lofty examples of self sacrifice committed by you or people you know. Even if they're below the level of a Mother Teresa, they could still rank right up there with such acts as rescuing a person or animal from a burning building or giving up food so that another might eat.

You can take the opposite approach and write about something mundane, such as driving. For instance, do you drive and talk on the phone? Of course you do. Can you check your messages, send a fax, and redesign your webpage, all while cutting across three lanes of traffic? Shame on you. Hang up and drive.

Often, insight involves the act of experiencing something that triggers a memory. My use of the word "experiencing" was intentional, preferable to a more limiting term, such as "seeing." The inspiration might indeed come from something seen, but might just as easily be something experienced through your other senses.

You see the face of a stranger that reminds you of your fifth grade teacher.

You hear a piece of music that whisks you back to your prom or honeymoon.

You pet a dog or get sand between your toes, and the tactile sensation acts as a time machine.

You taste a dessert that is just like your mother used to make.

Or – the strongest memory trigger of all – you smell something. Maybe it's the aroma of freshly ground coffee or vanilla extract or burning leaves. It doesn't matter what smell triggers a given memory, some smells are strong enough to pick us up and carry us away. (More on memories in chapter five.)

Investigation: Check It Out.

This is the research part of the process, considered by many to be the most interesting. Now that you have your idea, you must find the facts to support it. These facts come from such sources as interviews, family records, and your own memories. See chapter six for interviewing techniques.

Internalization: Let It Cook.

Don't try to write right away. The creation of many of our favorite delectables, from Chardonnay to sauerkraut, requires a fermentation process. Never mind the chemistry involved in these processes; it is simply a time when the ingredients are changing and finding their proper or intended relation to each other. After you have saturated yourself with facts, those facts need time to find their proper places relative to each other. There is no timetable for how long it will take. You're ready when you're ready.

Rush at your own risk. One of the dangers in writing too soon is the possibility of misplaced emphasis. You might choose to devote more space to one aspect of your story simply because you know more about it than you do the other aspects. But that part of the story could end up being a subordinate section. It's too early in the process to know what part each fact will play. One word of warning: when in doubt, write it down. You might not use it, but it's there if you need it. Another benefit: having written these thoughts down, you'll be more aware of how you feel about them.

In short, write when you feel the urge. However, the facts you have learned will generally need some time to sort themselves out.

Inspiration: Let It Out.

You might think that inspiration should be first on the list. "I'm inspired to write something because of a memory, a face, a piece of music, etc." No, it *occurs* to you to begin the writing process, but you're not truly *inspired* to craft sentences, to shape paragraphs, and in general, to tell the story. The latter doesn't happen until you have internalized the facts and those facts have found one another and everything is ready to erupt.

Be ready. An idea for a phrase or other way of saying something can breeze in like a bachelor uncle, then vanish in an instant. Be ready to record. Have a notebook or tape recorder handy… always. At home. At work. In the car. On the bedside table. Those of you with control issues will hate this part, because you have absolutely no say in when all those internalized facts, having sufficiently fermented, will bubble to the surface. Get over it and record.

Warning: people who don't write don't understand this need to record fleeting ideas and phrases the instant — or soon after — they occur. If you're with someone and an idea comes to you and you jot it down, they'll probably say, "Are you writing about me?" Even if you aren't, say yes and then watch their reaction. It's fun.

Implementation: Write It Down.

Keep reading; this is what the rest of the book is about.

These five steps constitute the writing process. Do yourself a favor and follow all of them. Skipping steps is like a banana going directly from green to brown. Then you'd be writing banana bread instead of bananas.

Chapter 1
Structure and Point of View

You can tell many of your true stories using fictional structure and controlled point of view. Structure means the order in which you tell the events of your story. Point of view refers to how you let the reader view the events of the story.

Most writers start at the beginning of the story and write toward the end simply because that's the way events unfold. This method is born of a long and noble tradition, having been first codified by the Greek philosopher Aristotle more than 2,300 years ago. It was a Tuesday, it was raining, and he had nothing else to do, so he established the enduring and deceptively simple concept of beginning, middle, and end.

To paraphrase his description, before the beginning there is nothing and after the end there is nothing. That sounds a bit metaphysical, but he simply meant that before the story begins nothing happens that we need to know about, nor after the end of the story. It doesn't matter whether you're describing a life-altering event or an illuminating anecdote. All the events in the story are self-contained. Read the following anecdote, and then we'll dissect it.

The Story

I was a missing person when I was three ... according to Mom.

We were a slightly extended household in the small town of New Brighton, Pennsylvania, in the summer of 1952. My father's sister, my Aunt Bea, lived with us then, so that made four of us. My father worked in a factory not far from our two-bedroom house. Aunt Bea was a young, single woman working in an office. Since her name was Beatrice, her family nickname was Beedee. But at three years of age, I had trouble pronouncing that, so to me she was "Aunt BB." She drove a big black 1936 Chevy, but she took the bus to work, leaving her car in our ramshackle garage. My mother was a housewife, back when it was still permissible to use that term. I held down a full-time job as a toddler.

One morning, Dad and Aunt Bea were at work, and Mom was home with me. She was cleaning upstairs when she realized she couldn't hear me. In fact, she hadn't heard me for a while. She looked in both bedrooms and the bathroom; I wasn't there. She looked downstairs in the dining room, living room and kitchen. No me. The basement door was locked, and the latch was too high for me to reach, so she knew I couldn't be down there.

Her unease building, Mom looked in the back yard. Not there. The front yard. Still nothing. She knocked on the door of our elderly neighbor, Mrs. Heinzig. I wasn't there, nor had Mrs. Heinzig seen me. Panic at a peak now, she called our other next-door neighbor, a young man named Jim. As Jim stepped over the low fence that separated our two properties, my mother ran to him, crying. "I can't find Jay!"

"Don't worry," Jim said. "We'll find him."

They glanced at the garage and its weathered wood and flaking paint, but the side door was closed, a small wooden peg securing the lock's hasp. As with the basement door, I couldn't have gotten in there either.

They scoured the rest of the neighborhood, knocking on door after door, but no one had seen me. By this time, Mom had passed panic. She and Jim returned to the back yard, simply because there was nowhere else to look. Then my mother noticed the big garage doors.

Aunt Bea's Chevy was long, and the garage was old, so old that it was too short for the car. When the car was parked in the garage, the doors would close only part way, not quite touching the back bumper. This resulted in a small gap. Mom and Jim pulled the doors open and entered the gloom of the garage.

They moved to the side window of the car and there I was, calmly sitting in the back seat. I looked up at the two relieved faces and happily informed them, "I go in BB's car."

The Breakdown

We like the number 3. We love and need the number 3. Look at all the things that come in threes: wishes, blind mice, stooges. Jokes are structured in three parts, the two-part setup and the snapper. "A priest, a minister, and a rabbi walk into a bar..." Guaranteed, if you try to write a joke about a priest, a minister, a rabbi, and an ayatollah, it wouldn't work. It's the same with the three-act structure in script writing and the beginning-middle-end in story telling. Even a one-act play has a beginning, a middle, and an end, structurally.

There's a writer's rule of thumb about structure:
Get your hero up a tree, throw stones at him, then get him down.

26

Problem is introduced, problem gets worse, problem is resolved.

Can't find child, can't find child *anywhere*, find child.

Beginning, middle, and end. Read any conventionally plotted novel or watch any TV show or see any mass-market American movie, and 999 times out of a thousand, you'll find this structure if you look for it. The reader or viewer expects three parts, and if you want your story to resonate structurally, you'd better accommodate.

The first line of the story was to get your attention. Onward.

In the rest of the setup, I wanted to provide enough details to allow you to paint a picture in your mind and still not overburden you with minutiae. What details did I provide? No matter what year you read this, you know how old I am now since I was three in 1952. You know our immediate family structure and living arrangements. The detail of my aunt's 16-year-old car says as much about economic circumstances as about how they built cars in those days. Really, what more do we need?

(One important fact not in evidence is that my mother was a very conscientious parent. She misplaced me only that one time.)

In the beginning of the story, I had to accomplish three things:

1) Introduce the characters. Who is the story about and who takes part in it? My mother, our neighbor Jim, and, offstage for most of the action, yours truly.

2) Establish the setting. Where are we and when are we? A modest house in a small Pennsylvania town in 1952.

3) Establish the problem or issue at hand. A child is missing.

In the middle, the problem gets worse or more com-

27

plicated; this is known as "rising action." Complications and reversals arise, exacerbating the problem. Not only can my mother not find me in the house, she can't find me outside in the front or back yard, at the neighbors' houses, or anywhere in the neighborhood. Fiction writers talking shop will speak of conflict, and, being human, we find conflict interesting (other people's conflict anyway; we don't like it when it happens to us). In our equation, conflict = problem, and no problem = no interest. The conflict doesn't need to be a war; it can just be someone seeking something or someone, and being unable to immediately achieve that goal.

Not all events contain rising action, but if you structure it properly, your story will seem to have a middle. Do not make up details! Just tell us what happened by starting slowly. Introduce a minor aspect of the main problem first, then move to the knottier parts of the problem, then, finally, the solution.

In the end, we have the resolution wherein the problem is resolved. Mom and Jim find me in Aunt Bea's car. In some cases, the problem might not be completely solved, but some kind of closure is achieved. Many times in life – too many, sadly – problems drag on and on and seem never to come to a resolution. Note: If the series of events does not have a conclusion, it's not a story. You can certainly include these events in your memoirs, but if too many situations are still hanging fire, maybe you shouldn't be writing your life story yet.

Point Of View
Through whose eyes do we see the action unfold?

Point of view is closely allied with structure – and sometimes even dictates the structure. Point of view refers to the eyes through which we see the events of the story play out. The writer of pure fiction has more choices than the memoir writer in this area because the former is making things up, but the latter is bound by all those pesky facts and actual occurrences. Consequently, you the memoir writer have the harder job, because the stories you're telling are factual. At least they'd better be.

The memoir writer has three choices for point of view:

Objective/Omniscient: a detached narrator tells the story, but takes no part in it. The two versions of this technique are:

1)   Objective: a camera's eye, fly-on-the-wall POV, describes events with no internal investigation of the thoughts and emotions of the participants, and

2)   Omniscient: the narrator can see into people's heads to describe their surface thoughts and emotions.

For instance, let's say you're telling a story about someone other than you, and that someone becomes ill. Using the objective technique, you can describe only the external evidence of the person's illness; you can't get inside.

> John's face glowed a sickly shade of green and he groaned as he clutched his stomach and doubled over.

Using the omniscient technique, a fiction writer might say:

> John felt his face grow hot and sweaty, and his stomach lurched and growled; breakfast was on the rise!

Using the omniscient POV, you can jump from the inside of one person's head to another, but it might become a bit confusing for the reader.

> In the insurance office that Monday morning, John's stomach was feeling queasy, Mary was worried about

whether her car would pass inspection, and old Mrs. McPherson thought that John and Mary would make a lovely couple.

Remember, the O/O POV works well for telling someone else's story. In writing your own story, however, you will probably have limited need for this technique, as the majority of the stories in the memoir will involve you. For that reason, you'll probably use...

First person: a description of events told from a personal POV involving events that you yourself participated in. You'll use the pronouns *I*, *me*, and *my*. Of all the characters who are involved in your story, the only person whose thoughts and internal emotions you may describe are your own. This is for an obvious reason: you're not a mind reader. And if you did attribute even obvious emotions to people in the story, it would ring false. In the example where John gets sick, you could write it from a first person POV in which you observe John becoming sick, but you would use the first example, external evidence. It would be your observations of John's distress. On the other hand, if you were the one getting sick, you could go internal, but please, spare us the details.

Limited third person: you might use this technique when you're telling someone else's story, such as a relative, an ancestor, or a friend. This POV is similar to objective/omniscient; the difference is that with limited third person, you are still using the third person pronoun, he or she, but *you're limiting the viewpoint to that one person*. Writers may also describe that person's thoughts and emotions, but the main point of this method is what the point-of-view person knows.

Who described Sherlock Holmes's exploits to us? Dr. Watson, of course. Holmes was the protagonist, the character whose actions drive the story. Arthur Conan Doyle used a first-person narrator to describe *Watson's observations* of how Holmes solved his cases.

Sherlock Holmes had nearly superhuman observational and deductive abilities. At a crime scene, Holmes could look at a single animal hair through his magnifying glass and tell you that the hair was from a dog, half Maltese and half bulldog, that the dog's owner's name is Fred and Fred's great-great grandmother walked with a limp and spoke French. Dr. Watson would stand there wide-eyed, and exclaim, "How extraordinary, Holmes!" And so, vicariously, would we. (I'm exaggerating Holmes's powers, but not by much.)

Watson represented us, the non-investigator with only normal deductive powers. If Conan Doyle had used Holmes as the viewpoint character (which he did only once, to poor effect, in "The Adventure of the Blanched Soldier"), most stories would have been over in a page and a half because we would see everything Holmes saw all at once, and there goes the mystery.

I'm referring to the Watson of the stories written by Conan Doyle, not the 40s-era movies with Basil Rathbone as Holmes and the fine actor, Nigel Bruce, as Watson. In these films, Bruce portrayed Watson as an amiable dolt who was totally befuddled by Holmes's deductions. Conversely, Conan Doyle's literary Watson was an intelligent, perceptive physician, perfect for the reader to identify with. Wouldn't you rather identify with a smart person than a buffoon? Besides, if Watson was smart and still couldn't see what Holmes could, that meant Holmes was even smarter.

My missing person anecdote is told, for the most part, from my mother's point of view because I have no memory of the incident, only her retelling of the story. In fact, when I was writing it, the images in my head were created by my mother's telling of the story, not by my own memories. Yes, I use the first person pronoun "I", but only for background information and necessary references to me. Besides, if the story were told from my POV, there would be no tension.

> One day when I was 3, I wandered
> out to our garage and sat in the back
> seat of my Aunt Bea's car. Boy, was
> my mother relieved when she finally
> found me.

Not exactly a nail-biter, is it?

The fiction writer has another choice, and that is second person, "you." The writer says things like "You walk into your office and find your potted plant is on fire." This is intended to provide immediacy and a sense of you-are-there for the reader. Most writers don't do this because mostly it doesn't work. It's artificial and intrusive, and besides, *you* know you didn't do those things. So don't even think about it.

Here's a way to help you decide on person and point of view. Imagine the reader asking you one question after reading your story: How do you know? That will keep you out of other characters' heads, where you don't belong.

Present or Past Tense

Verb tense plays a strong part in story telling, and the choice of tense can affect the reader's perception and enjoyment of the story. Use past tense in writing; use either past or present in oral storytelling.

Past tense is preferable for the page. After all, the events you're relating have already happened (you know, in the *past*); therefore, past tense is the better choice. To my mind's ear, a piece of fiction written in present tense has a kind of forced immediacy. Try as I might, I cannot forget that these events supposedly already happened, and are not in fact happening at the moment I read about them. And that serves to pull me out of the story, if indeed I was ever in it in the first place. A true story written in the present tense suffers for the same reason.

However, a true story told orally in the present tense – if it's well done – can be exciting for the listener. Go figure.

Bonus Extra: Progressive Disclosure

Progressive disclosure is a fancy term for doling out each bit of information in its own good time.

I withheld some important information in the early part of the anecdote: as my mother glanced at the side door of the garage and saw that the latch was secure, I didn't mention the fact that the big garage doors could not be closed over the bumper of the car, leaving the small opening. You would have figured it out. Was I cheating in withholding that fact? You might argue with me, but I say no. Because those doors were closed as far as they could be, to the members of our family those doors were effectively "closed." Or *our version* of closed. And besides, this story is told from the POV of a worried mother desperately looking for her missing only child. If you were in her position, you might miss that little detail, too.

To help you decide what to disclose when:

1. Make a list of the important events of your story.

2. Number them chronologically.

3. Decide which ones you need to withhold until later in the story or the end.

When making these decisions about progressive disclosure, don't be in a rush to tell everything all at once. You like to be surprised when you read a story, don't you? So will your readers.

Knowing structure, voice/POV, verb tense, and progressive disclosure might seem like technical aspects of writing that professional writers need to know. Well, they are, but using them to write your life stories will make the organization of them much easier.

Journal/Notes

Journal/Notes

Journal/Notes

Journal/Notes

Chapter 2
Description
Writing for the inner ear and the mind's eye

We're a pretty interesting species, we *Homo sapiens sapiens*. Latter-day hunter-gatherers, we're a visual species, with eyes perfectly designed for focusing in on game (the hunter) or casting our gaze wider when foraging for edible vegetation and watching for predators (the gatherer). What our eyes are not as well designed for is reading, and yet we do quite a lot of it.

We're just as visual in our mind's eye. When we read, we love to see pictures in our minds, and the right words help us paint those pictures. Think of the last novel you read. Can you see the scenes that the writer wrote for you? If it was well written, you can. Consider this: of you and all the other people who read that same novel, no two of you saw exactly the same pictures in your heads. And yet if it was written to include enough pertinent details, every reader created the same generally appropriate imagery.

We're also eavesdroppers. Studies have shown that audience members viewing an instructional video retain more information from illustrative, dramatized scenes than from an on-screen spokesperson simply telling them the information. That's because when the audience members are watching the actors in a dramatized situation, they are figuratively eavesdropping. Any number of film deconstructionists have pointed out Alfred Hitchcock's view that all audiences are voyeurs in the sense of being prying observers of other people's lives, and the movie screen is the audience's window. In fact, many of Hitchcock's films begin with a shot through a window, e.g., *Psycho* and *Rope*. In *Rear Window*, Jimmy Stewart spends the entire movie looking out his window and into Raymond Burr's.

Meanings of Meanings

Writing is a series of arcane processes that somehow leads to words on a page. Consider: you're attempting to take your nonlinear goulash of thoughts, memories, and mental impressions and shape them into a linearly expressed story. Yikes, you're thinking, maybe this is a lost cause. It isn't; people do it all the time. But you must realize that even the best, most carefully chosen words are only an approximate translation of your thoughts and memories. And every translation is flawed.

The most precise translation from one language to another will be an inexact match between cultures. Even the simple word "now" has connotation issues. In English, the word is just a syllable, relating to nothing more than the reader's or listener's concept of *now*. It comes from the Latin *nunc*, cascading through various Germanic languages as *nu*, finally becoming our familiar *now*. To English speakers, the word has no relation to any other thing or concept. On the other hand, the French word for

39

now is *maintenant*, from the words *main*, hand, and the verb *tenir*, to hold. So for the French, the word has a subliminal quality of immediacy, of something that is so present, so *now*, that it can be held in the hand.

In English, we fare a little better when it comes to meals. Breakfast is easy: we're breaking our fast. In French, the term is *le petit dejeuner*. The word *jeuner* means to fast, so if we de-*jeuner*, we're not fasting any more. The noun *dejeuner* actually means lunch, but let's not get into that. In German, breakfast is *Frühstück*: *früh* means early and *stück* means piece or bit. As you can see, all these words relate more or less directly with their concepts.

But with half a million words catalogued in the Oxford English Dictionary, the problem of disassociation is touchy within this language. Subtle shadings of meaning abound in a language with such multifarious origins of words to describe the same concept. Because people carry around their individual cultures like high school students schlepping their backpacks, they also carry around individual connotations for words. For that reason, writers must be careful to use words that provide enough information that the important facts will be understood. For instance:

The dog ran into the house.

Not much to go on, is there? A sentence with such limited descriptors forces you to supply your own imagery, probably your favorite dog and style of house. What did you see? Terrier? Chihuahua? Great Dane? Lhasa Apso? What kind of house? Split level? Colonial? Dog house? Scarlett O'Hara's Tara? (Before we go any further, I acknowledge that there are always a few skewed souls who envision the poor pooch crashing into the side of the house rather than racing through the open front door.) If the details are important, be specific.

The brindle dachshund ran into the
Tudor mansion.

Be specific the right way: limit your use of modifiers. We all know that adjectives are modifiers of nouns. Look up the word modify in the dictionary and you'll find "to change," but you'll also find "to limit." That's the grammatical definition, to limit the way the reader perceives the word that is being modified.

The man entered the room.

This sentence does not have nearly enough data for the reader to form a fleshed out image. Try this:

The tall man hurried into the dining
room.

Better, but let's be more specific.

The janitor ran into the classroom.
The doctor strode into the boardroom.

We're getting warmer. Now we can provide even more details, thereby fleshing out the reader's mental movie.

Mr. Polhaus, the janitor, ran into the
classroom and asked the kindergar-
ten students to lift their feet so he
could mop the floor.

Dr. Polhaus, the eminent vascular
surgeon, strode into the boardroom,
faced the board of directors, and an-
nounced that he had bought the hos-
pital.

Don't force your readers to wade through a string of modifiers.

> The short, portly, well-dressed, limping man entered the office.

Actually, that's not wading: it's more like swimming under water and coming up for air when you finally reach the noun. Try redistributing your adjectives over a few additional sentences.

> Mr. Polhaus favored his injured right leg as he hobbled into the psychologist's office. His lemon yellow Armani suit was impeccably tailored to his stocky, 5'4" frame, but he still looked like a freshly painted fireplug.

If the previous description is a little too Raymond Chandler for you, feel free to dial yours down a notch or two.

If you're planning to describe someone, do so immediately or not at all. If you wait until page five of a ten-page story to tell us that Mr. Polhaus had blond hair, a crew cut, and a goatee, that's too late. The reader has already formed an image of Mr. Polhaus, and odds are it's different from yours. This will result in the cardinal sin of writing: pulling the reader out of the story.

As a reader, you are pulled into a story and held by the most fragile of threads. You might be so involved in a story that you feel you're a part of it. The story is so engrossing that you even forget that you're reading. But all it takes is one misstep by the writer – an anachronism, a typo, a delayed description – and those gossamer threads break. Suddenly you're not in the story any more. You're thrown out into the cold, cruel world and looking at words on a page. The writer has betrayed you.

In the last example, I used one of the great tools of the writer, the simile, in which something is compared to something else, i.e. Mr. Polhaus and the fireplug. It helps visualization and it can be entertaining if the writer is not too heavy-handed.

The metaphor is similar to the simile, but with a crucial difference: where the simile says something is *like* something else, the metaphor says that something *is* something else, figuratively speaking. In the simile, Mr. Polhaus is like a fireplug. The metaphor: Polhaus was a fireplug of a man.

Simile: He fought like a tiger during the negotiations.

Metaphor: During the negotiations, he was a tiger for the points he favored and a mule for the points he hated.

Tiger and mule have their clichéd connotations of ferocity and stubbornness, respectively. For just that reason, you need to be aware of the emotional clout in the words you choose. For instance, compare *skinny* and *slender*. Both words have the same intent: describing a human body with very little fat. The first word is negative, the second, positive. Tread carefully.

Closely related to the metaphor and the simile is the analogy. The analogy, however, implies that only *part* of something is like something else. The word comes from the Greek meaning *proportion*. Refer to the introduction, where the writing process is compared to the banana. Obviously writing is not completely like a banana, otherwise writing would be yellow, would grow on tropical trees, and would be frowned upon by Atkins dieters.

Two Methods of Description: Time and Space
Description can be temporal (time-related) or spa-

43

tial (space-related). Temporal description is the simpler and easier of the two. It's describing events or procedures in the order in which they happened. Or, in the case of a procedure, the order in which events *should* happen.

We tell entire stories temporally, in the order in which events unfolded. First A happens, then B happens, which causes C, D, and E to happen, then everybody lives happily ever after. Yet within those stories, we can describe people, places, things, and events using a combination of temporal and spatial techniques.

We give directions to someone's house temporally. "Go five miles along Route 9, then turn left at Miller's Hardware, then go another eight miles and turn left at the intersection where the Sunoco station used to be." Don't skip any steps in the description or the process will fail, i.e., people will get lost.

Recipes in cookbooks are temporally written. "First, separate two eggs. Then melt a tablespoon of butter. Then bring the eggs back together again along with a cup of flour, add the melted butter, and beat until smooth." You're writing directions for a procedure, directions which must be followed in sequence. Don't skip any steps in the description or the process will fail, i.e., the food will be inedible.

You have no choices in variation with the temporal method; either you relate the events or procedures in sequence or you don't. However, many more choices exist in the spatial method.

You're describing the house you grew up in. Where do you start, with the slate roof and work your way down, or with the foundation and work your way up? Your choice, but be consistent. Maybe neither the roof nor the foundation is very interesting, so you opt for a distinctive feature of the house. Whatever you do, decide on a starting point and a direction. Don't jump from the leaded glass window on the second floor to the ornamental doorknob on the back door to the swing on the front porch.

You want to paint a mental picture for the readers, not give them whiplash.

Do you start with the inside and work your way out, or vice versa? Again, it's your choice; just be consistent. This method is for detailed descriptions, not a cursory sketch. If you want to limit your description to "Victorian painted lady" or "1950s split level," you needn't worry about spatial concerns.

The same criteria apply to descriptions of such things as landscapes. You can start by describing the fallen leaves at your feet, then move to the burbling brook full of hyperactive trout, to the amber waves of grain on the other side of the brook, ending with the distant mountain range under a cerulean blue sky. Or you could start at a distance and work your way closer. Same rule: Be consistent.

Negatives: What Not to Show.

We are such a visual species that even little black marks on a page are turned into images. We're so eager to see pictures in our minds that we see even what we're not supposed to.

For instance:

Let's say you're writing about a childhood adventure, the time you explored that cave you were explicitly told to avoid. Deep in the cave, your flashlight's batteries die. Some people would express the result as:

Suddenly there was no light in the cave.

What's wrong with that phrasing? While the facts are accurate, you're using a term for a concept you do not want the reader to envision: light. Here's what happens in the reader's mind. For a split second, they see light, then they realize, oops, no light, not supposed to see light, turn it off. By then it's too late, they've seen the light. Better phrasing:

45

Suddenly, the cave was plunged into total darkness.

Sometimes, though, the use of negatives can work to the writer's advantage. Take this sentence:

The old woman opened her refrigerator and saw that there was no food.

You want the reader to be involved in your story, and that involvement should be emotional. If we want to create sympathy for the destitute senior, what better way than to create the fleeting image of food, only to take it away?

Senses

Just as we can use our senses to revive dormant memories, writers can use sensory-based descriptors to help their readers produce their mental movies. Mostly we write about how things look. In fact, the majority of your description will be visual because we're primarily a visual species. But don't completely ignore the other four senses.

It's raining.

You can *look* out the window and describe the way the driving, gray deluge produces cascades of water that warp and ripple the image of your dog racing toward the front door.

Describe the *sound* as the rain batters the window.

The *feeling* of the cool needle-tingle of rain on your face when you open the door to let the dog in...

The clean *taste* as you lick the water off your lips...

The *smell* of ozone as lightning cracks just overhead.

And remember that sometimes no analogies, metaphors, or similes are necessary. A wet dog smells like nothing except a wet dog.

Think of description not as providing a photograph for your readers, delineating every minute detail, but rather as a sketch of what you want their mind's eye to depict. Far from being a solitary art, writing is a collaboration, a partnership with the reader. You the writer are not taking the description all the way to the reader; you're meeting the reader halfway. Good reading is a participatory act, with the reader doing some of the work in creating the mental movies. Avoid over-describing; leave the reader something to do.

Don't write with a thesaurus at your side, either. The direct statement, written in standard, precise, unembellished language, is usually the best. But we need variety, so spice up your prose, to taste. These are your stories, so make it your voice, not the voice you'd like it to be or that you think your readers expect.

It is doubtful that a precise correlation between image and word will ever happen, neither between your thoughts and your words, nor between your words and the reader's mental movies that are created by your words.

Write anyway.

Chapter 3
Distilled Conversation

"Here's lookin' at you, kid."
"I'll make him an offer he can't refuse."
"What we have here is a failure to communicate."

Good dialogue sticks with us. It's beneficial for people, both the real and the fictional. Good dialogue makes fictional characters come alive, and it draws out a fundamental characteristic of readers as human beings: we love eavesdropping on what other people say, even when we know their words are made up.

In novels and movies, dialogue is not conversation; it only sounds like it. Conversation is real, but dialogue is made up. As a memoir writer, you're telling true stories, so you'll need a combination of the two. We'll take the best of both worlds and use the term "distilled conversation."

Fictional dialogue is artificial conversation with the nonessential filler removed. In real life, when we run into a friend or an acquaintance, we recite the litany:

"How are you?"

"Fine, thanks. You?"

"Can't complain. Nobody listens anyway."

"Ha ha."

"Ha ha."

You'll never hear such dialogue in a well-written movie because the previous exchange is all fluff and noise with no content and no purpose except to establish a rudimentary connection between two sentient, carbon-based bipeds.

You can make your true occurrences seem truer with the artful use of distilled conversation. Whereas fictional dialogue has two specific jobs, to reveal character and move the action along, real-life conversation has a multitude of general, nonspecific effects. In real life, conversation certainly can reveal character and provide information, but that isn't all it does. In fact, it often does not accomplish those things. True conversation can inform, enlighten, reveal, anger, entertain, incite, placate, seduce, energize, enervate, connect, divide, repulse, heal, wound … the effects go on.

Mostly, conversation connects people; it's how we learn about each other. Sometimes conversation even contains stories, but unfortunately not all conversations sparkle with wit. They often simply fill awkward silences with awkward and banal words, but at least they're noise. Where nature abhors a vacuum, Americans abhor a conversational lull. We'll fill it with anything. Weather. Sports scores. Gas mileage. But this noise does not belong in your stories.

Distilled conversation should be interesting; everyday conversation is often boring, even if it's your own. Sparkling conversation is a pleasure to eavesdrop on, but sadly most consist of recitations of what someone else said. Eavesdrop at the mall sometime.

> He goes "Get out of here," and I'm like "Whoa, dude, no way," and then he's all "You're so ten minutes ago."

Riveting. In your stories, distill your remembered conversations down to the essential content and lose the fluff.

Many fiction writers put dialogue on the very first page of a novel or short story to get the reader's attention immediately. Those quotation marks tell us that two people are talking, and with that comes the opportunity for the reader to eavesdrop. "Listen in," the quotation marks say, "you might hear something juicy."

In novels, some dialogue might seem like inane conversation, but if it's well crafted, it will reveal character and move the plot by revealing information ... even by what a person does not say.

In 1962, the Profumo/Keeler story broke. The scandal concerned British War minister John Profumo's relationship with London call girl Christine Keeler, who also had a relationship with a Soviet spy. The sex and state secrets scandal made all the papers and news broadcasts; some stories used the term call girl and others used prostitute. I was 13 then and asked my mother what a prostitute was. She went into a five-minute story about how she once asked an embarrassing question and how ill at ease it made her at the time. It wasn't until later that I realized she hadn't answered my question. (I was both a sheltered child and none too quick on the uptake.) The fact that she sidestepped my question illustrates an aspect of her character: illicit sex was not something to chat about in casual conversation, especially not to your child.

Form and function

Distilled conversation can take two forms, direct attribution and summary. Direct attribution relates the exact words people spoke, while summary dialogue gives us the gist without the actual spoken words.

Direct:
> Joan stood in the doorway of the family room and watched her husband read the paper. "That's all you do," she said, "read the paper and watch television. Oh yes, and eat." She took a deep breath. "I want a divorce."

Summary:
> Joan walked into the room and told her husband that she wanted a divorce.

We readers get much less emotional depth in the summary example because we don't get to hear Joan's exact words at this time of emotional crisis, words that explain her reasons and emotions. I could have written more about her inner feelings and emotions, but that's a little too fiction-like. I'm not inside her head. How would I know her actual emotions? (Of course, if Joan were writing this story, she could give us much more insight.)

Summary dialogue works fine for summarizing a conversation about a series of events.

> Six-year-old Billy told his mother about his day at school: reading aloud, arithmetic at the blackboard, and skinning his knee at recess.

The average child takes many more words to tell of events than are truly necessary, even though the words are invariably entertaining. This is also true of many adults, except for the entertaining part.

The two main tasks of dialogue manifest themselves in nonfiction as well as fiction.

Advance the story:
Wife: "I want a divorce."

Reveal character:
Husband (nose buried in the newspaper): "Mmm-hm. What's for lunch?"

Use distilled conversation to describe action. It can often paint pictures just as well as description can. As we read their spoken words, we see the action the words represent.

"Pass the jelly."
"Drop that gun!"
"Why are you limping?"

The Technical Aspects of Distilled Conversation

Attribution

Tacking "he said" and "she said" before or after the spoken words is called attribution. The spoken words are attributed to particular people. The slang term is "tag." Nine hundred and ninety-nine times out of a thousand, "said" is the only verb you will need in your tags. In my fiction classes, students have asked me about repeating a word too many times, and the question using the word "said" in the tags always comes up. It's okay to use it repeatedly because the reader doesn't sound it out mentally anyway. Notice this when you read your next novel; you sound out the dialogue in your head, but I'll bet you skip the tags.

Beginning writers try to add variety to attribution by thinking up alternatives to "said." A couple of variations will work, but don't bother racking your brain for others.

...he asked. (quite all right)

...he replied. (acceptable)

...he queried. (nope)

...he expostulated. (come on now)

Writers go to great lengths to add variety to their tags without adding common sense. "That's really funny," he laughed. Try laughing your words; it can't be done. "You get out of here and don't ever come back!" she hissed. Try hissing a sentence that doesn't have one "s" in it.

Use one paragraph per speaker. This keeps the reader on track as to who is speaking if you don't always use a tag. Even if speaker number one gives an entire speech and speaker two gives a one-word response, that one word is dropped down to the next line and indented and surrounded by quotation marks.

If only two people are talking, you don't need attribution for each person every time. Alternation refers to the back and forth nature of dialogue, and the reader keeps track by whose turn it is. Be careful though; even seasoned writers have been known to forget who's next in the speaking queue and attribute the wrong line to the wrong person.

Variations of Attribution

Use an action insert or an action pause in order to make your attribution more informative. This technique gives the speaker a bit of business to perform in place of the attribution. In addition to our mind's ear hearing what he says, our mind's eye gets to watch him do something.

Action insert:

"I want a divorce," said Joan.

"That's nice." Ralph turned the page of the newspaper. "What's for lunch?"

Action pause:

An action pause still uses the verb "said," but also

53

includes action.

> "I want a divorce," said Joan.
> "That's nice," Ralph said, un-
> buckling his galoshes. "What's for
> lunch?"

A note on punctuation: In direct attribution, quotation marks always enclose the speaker's words, and a
comma always separates the speaker from his/her words.
But we need to make a distinction. When the dialogue
tag comes at the end of the sentence, the comma falls inside the quotation marks. When the tag is at the beginning of the sentence, the comma falls outside the quotes.

> "You're beautiful," he said.

> He said, "You're beautiful."

Remember that no quotes are needed for summary
dialogue/ indirect discourse.

> He said that she was beautiful.

Distilled conversation in your stories should be
sparse, just enough to add flavor. It's the Worcestershire
sauce, not the steak. Most of your stories will tell what
someone did or what happened to someone, not what
someone said. Sure, they'll say things along the way, but
the focus will be on what happened. (See chapter one for
the missing person story and chapter seven for the bridge
story). Besides, it's unnatural for anyone to be able to remember long stretches of conversation verbatim. The written dialogue might be interesting, but it will be suspect.
You want your reader to trust you.

Journal/Notes

Journal/Notes

Journal/Notes

Journal/Notes

Chapter 4
Characterization:
Who are you? And please provide examples.

Characterization is the external manifestation of a personality demonstrated by attitudes, actions, and words. Looks are not characterization.

> John looked like Shaquille O'Neal,
> only taller.

While this sentence puts you on the road toward a physical description (with a long way yet to go), it tells you nothing of his personality. The reader needs more to go on. Use the following handy designations when considering how to describe both yourself and the other people who populate your stories.

Facets and Aspects

I use these two terms to illuminate the external and internal characteristics that make up a person. *Facets* refer to the various sides of ourselves that we present to the world and to the people we encounter. *Aspects* refer to the personal, inherent characteristics that make us what we are.

No one is only one thing. We start our lives with few facets, but as we move through our days, we take on additional roles, thereby growing multidimensional. You might not have all the following facets, but everybody has at least some of them. Your story should ideally embrace all the facets that make you *you*.

You, the parent. How do you relate to your children, if you have any? Are you the strict disciplinarian or the laissez-faire buddy? By the way, if you think you're clueless and out of your depth, welcome to the club. And if you're like many parents, you find yourself saying things your own parents said to you. (My favorite example of parental logic: Stop crying or I'll give you something to cry about. I'm still working on that one.)

You, the spouse/partner. Even if you're not married, you have probably been a partner in a relationship. Be honest; how well or poorly did you fare in relation to a significant other?

You, the son or daughter. I don't care if you have biological parents, foster/adoptive parents, or you were raised by wolves, somewhere in your days you had a parental figure to deal with. Did you drive them mad, make them proud, or both?

You, the brother or sister. If you have siblings, you automatically have stories. Half-, step-, and adopted siblings certainly qualify. If you're an only child, as I am, e-mail me and we'll commiserate about what we missed.

You, the friend. Whom are you close to outside your family? What friendships have lasted and what haven't … and why? Stories abound in both situations.

60

You, the worker. At first blush, this might seem an odd facet to include in our self-description. But in this culture, you are what you do, and that facet of your personality is an important part of the whole package.

Our aspects are much more personal characteristics. They are the physical, mental, spiritual, and emotional parts of our character. Ponder how to define yourself...

Physically. What is your physical appearance? Do you have a feature that dominates? Hair, eyes, smile, height, physique, broad shoulders, big feet? Do you exercise or is your picture in the dictionary under "couch potato?"

Mentally. I'm not referring solely to years of education, although that's part of it, but to the way you think. How do you solve problems?

Spiritually. You can be spiritual and never set foot in a church or synagogue. Are you one with God or are you a child of the Universe? You can discuss your religion or your core beliefs. Spiritual also refers to paranormal occurrences. Have you ever seen a ghost? Do you even believe in them? For my version of spirituality, read the final chapter.

Emotionally. This aspect goes beyond getting teary at Hallmark commercials. What moves you deeply? What stirs you to feelings of love, anger, sympathy, antipathy. What scares you? What draws you? In short, what pushes your emotional buttons?

Personality Types

Elsewhere in this book, I mention that we like to categorize people. One popular way to do this lately is by personality types. This penchant for categorization has been around for awhile. Around 190 AD, the Roman physician Galen put forth an explanation of why people had such different personalities. He said (in Latin, of course) that a person's temperament was governed by a predominance of one of four bodily fluids, or humors (whence the word "humorous"). The "scientific" principle has been discarded, but Galen's classic terms survive: sanguine (governed by blood), choleric (yellow bile), melancholy (black bile), and phlegmatic (phlegm [sorry]).

Briefly, sanguines are the energetic extroverts, the people- and fun-oriented personalities. They aren't very well organized, but they are well liked. Choleric are the extroverted leaders, the motivators who not only get things done, they motivate others to get things done as well. Melancholic are the organizers and the organized, the sensitive and artistic introverts. The phlegmatic are introverted as well, and are the rocks in a relationship: steady, calm, reliable, and wryly humorous (there's that word again).

Most of us are blends of these qualities, but one quality will often dominate. I have found it helpful to think of people I've known as members of one of these four clubs.

Stories

When it comes to describing the personality of a person, all readers are from Missouri. You know, show me. The writer's adage "show, don't tell" stems from our readers' desires to have pictures painted in their minds.

For instance...

Men lie to each other, and half the time each participant in the exchange knows it.

Summer, 1967. Fresh out of high school, I was working a summer job in a steel mill, a subsidiary of the company my father worked for. They put me in the annealing section, where huge coils of thick wire were heat-treated, later to be formed into various small fittings such as rivets. My boss's name was Russell, and he was also foreman of the section and president of the union. In the capacity of president, Russell had dealings with the head of Personnel (what we call Human Resources today), a man named Charlie.

I was beginning my first career as a photographer in those days, and everybody knew it, so somebody at the company asked me to take pictures at the company picnic. When the photographs came back from the lab, I brought them to work, and the whole crew gathered around me to have a look, Russell included.

Then Russell saw Charlie walk through the entrance to the annealing bay, about 20 yards away, and head toward us. Russell quickly put the photos back in their envelope before Charlie was close enough to see. Charlie came over and asked if the pictures were back yet. Russell said they were, held up the envelope, and both men headed for Russell's office to look at them.

"Come on, Charlie," Russell said as they walked away. "You'll be the first one to see them."

Looking surprised, Charlie said, "Haven't you looked at them yet?"

Russell draped his arm around Charlie's shoulder. "No, Charlie, you'll be the first one."

Interesting, isn't it?

First of all, Russell hated Charlie because he was a member of management, and therefore an adversary of the union. And Charlie certainly didn't think highly of Russell, probably because of Charlie's feelings about union demands. Both men were engaged in this seemingly amoral dance of stroking and being stroked as a part of an understood pecking order. Charlie had more power, and Russell chafed at that.

What do these facts tell us about the men's characters and personalities? Both men knew precisely the unwritten rules of this dance. Charlie knew he was being lied to, and Russell knew that Charlie knew. Furthermore, I'm sure Charlie never asked if I had seen the photos, even though he knew full well that I was the photographer.

He was allowing the lie to pass unchallenged, probably because he liked the idea that Russell was kowtowing to him. But from what I remember of Russell, he wanted something. That was more than likely the reason for the soft soap. And from what I remember of Charlie, he knew it.

Russell's lie and Charlie's acceptance of it maintained this fragile relationship. If Charlie had challenged the lie, the bond would have been damaged. I don't believe Russell's action was a form of moral self-sacrifice, because Russell was obviously a practiced dissembler. But if he gave it any thought, he might have seen lying as being for the good of the union because he was keeping Charlie happy, the old "for the greater good" rationale.

Note on point of view: Writing the story from my POV lets the reader in on the deception and demonstrates the relationship between the two men. Nearly every word spoken was tantamount to a lie, even Charlie's feigned surprise that no one else had seen the photographs. Distilled conversation can indeed be untrue if it illustrates a point or relationship.

You might not think very highly of either of these men, but make no mistake: both Russell and Charlie thought they were righteous in their actions. No well-crafted, credible bad guy ever sees himself as a villain. Whatever their motives and rationalizations (and I admit that I'm making educated deductions as to their motives with room for error), we have witnessed their actions and can now make our own judgments.

We like to be shown, therefore...

Don't tell us he's stingy, show him leaving a dime tip for a ten-dollar lunch.

Don't tell us she's awkward, show her tripping over the pattern in the carpet.

Don't tell us he's brilliant, show him getting pi to come out even.

Don't tell us she's scatterbrained, show her driving five miles with her turn signal blinking.

Motives

We make determinations about people by *what* we see them do, but consider how much better we know the person when we understand the *why* of the person's actions. Provide us with these internal motivations, because they might show us a hidden facet of the person.

He isn't stingy, it was the last money he had and he wanted to leave something.

She isn't awkward, she has a balance problem.

He isn't brilliant, he cheats by rounding off.

She isn't scatterbrained, she's thinking of how to get *pi* to come out even without rounding off.

We're curious about people. This curiosity is a deeply rooted survival instinct. The more we know about a person, the better we are able to gauge the potential threat or lack thereof. We want this information even from the marks on the page because it helps us flesh out our mental picture.

Journal/Notes

Journal/ Notes

Journal/ Notes

Journal/Notes

•

Chapter 5
Memories

The palest ink is better than the best memory.
– *Chinese proverb*

Two of the primary statistics of interest to genealogists are date of birth and date of death. We writers, however, are concerned with the story-rich events that take place in between. If you're a genealogist, go ahead and crunch your numbers, but take the time to stop and remember the roses. But how do we retrieve the memories of those roses, and just how accurate are they?

We don't pay attention, and psychologist Carl Jung thought that was tragic, according to Rebecca Suhoza, psychology instructor at Pittsburgh's Point Park University. "If we paid attention, we would have much more profound memories than we typically do," says Suhoza. "[But] we're an externally driven society that does not value internal experiences, such as memory."

Memory is one of the four endopsychic functions posited by Jung, who believed that we are all striving for internal balance. Jung says that memory is one of the devices for achieving that balance. But how best to retrieve those memories?

The prospecting sites for memories can be divided the three time periods: era, episode, and event. You start with a large period of time and then gradually narrow your focus. Whether you're prospecting for your own memories or helping someone else retrieve theirs, this technique helps to zero in on lost events.

Era — first get back to the extended life period you want to explore. These are measured in years, possibly even decades. College years, marriage, the time it takes your teenage offspring to return a video. Shorter than the Bronze Age, but longer than your vacation to the Grand Canyon.

Episode — next localize the time even more to a particular extended happening. This could involve weeks or months. Now you can think of your trip to the Grand Canyon. Summer vacation during the grade school years. Temporary transfer to the Omaha branch.

Event — the most focused you can get. This is something that happened over a period of minutes or hours. This facet concerns a brief event that happened during a particular episode within a certain era.

Examples:
Era — high school.
Episode — football season senior year.
Event — scoring the winning touchdown in the final game.

Era — first house.
Episode — remodeling.
Event — plunging the house into a blackout while rewiring the kitchen.

71

Get yourself back to the relevant time period, then explore the things that happened then. Those happenings will lead you to still other happenings. You can also have a conversation with someone who shared those times with you. Conversation is a great "Oh, yeah" trigger, i.e., "Oh, yeah, remember the time when...?"

Triggers
Memory triggers are the instigators of memory, the resurrectors of lost times. Sometimes the memories are very close to the surface and reappear without much effort. Others are more deeply buried and require extended excavation.

Triggers are sensual in nature, and nine times out of ten, the sensual trigger will be visual. You see a face or a place that whisks you back to an earlier time. To mine for memories, I recommend traveling to where the memories were created (if possible), even if the primary memory trigger is gone.

My 19th century elementary school building was torn down in the late 20th century and replaced with a modern, low-slung, pre-fab horror that has been both an insurance office and a day care center. The original building is gone, but the neighborhood is still there: the single family houses with their nearly non-existent yards; the elm and maple trees, their roots buckling the sidewalks; the sloping hillside at the rear of the property, which we overlooked as we stood on the stone steps having our class pictures taken by Mr. Correll, the local photographer; the Presbyterian church half a block away, which we could see while posing if we looked a few degrees to the right,.

The sense of sight obviously applies to movies and TV as well, but it is also closely allied to the sense of hearing in that certain lines of dialogue and snatches of theme songs can act as triggers. Popular music of a given era can take you back, as can unpopular tunes.

Touch. The stone in your shoe or the feel of the

lips you're kissing.

Taste. Custard pie or castor oil.

Smell, the hair trigger of recall. From freshly baked bread to freshly cut grass, from farm to pharmacy, the olfactory sense is the hands down winner in the memory sweepstakes. For instance, I remember the smell of my parents' insurance agent, Mr. Rolls. (No, he didn't smell like baked goods.) He smoked and carried a leather satchel, in which he carried his ledger book, and the combined scents of tobacco and leather were indelibly imprinted in my six-year-old brain. Besides, he came to the house to collect the premium, and that just doesn't happen anymore. That's probably another reason I remember him; you tend to recall things that are radically different from the way they are today.

Dr. Nancy Mramor, a clinical psychologist specializing in mind/body/spirit issues, suggests that the sense of smell might be a strong trigger because it's an internalized sensation. "This is the only sense where something comes into the body without perceived physical contact," Mramor says. No other physical sensations are competing to divert our attention from the memory.

We can't ignore it either. We can turn off some of our other senses, depending on how occupied our minds are. We can ignore the sight of people around us, tune them out when they speak, but we can't not smell something.

Inaccurate Memories

Just because we remember something, that doesn't necessarily mean we're remembering it accurately. Consider the different forms of remembering:

1.) Voluntary memories and involuntary memories

2.) Remembering an event and remembering the story *about* an event

Rebecca Suhoza says the difference between vol-

73

untary and involuntary memories means a potential difference in the accuracy of those memories. Voluntary memories provide the potential for inaccuracies. "The ego is the person you think you are," says Suhoza. "When you're [consciously] remembering your past, you're distorting your past to fit your current reality."

I can find no better example than the story told by pioneering developmental psychologist Jean Piaget (1896-1980). He told of an event he remembered from his childhood of being saved from kidnappers by his nanny. Piaget told of details such as the scratches on his nanny's face from fighting off the would-be abductors. The only hitch in the accuracy of his memories is that the event never happened. The nanny made up the story, reportedly to get sympathy, and told Piaget the story when he was so young that he could not separate what was real from what he was told was real.

A similar, if less dramatic, memory quirk happened to me in the writing of this book. In the missing person story in chapter one, I wrote about the double garage doors that would not close completely because Aunt Bea's car was too long for the garage. When I originally wrote down notes on the story as I remembered my mother telling it, I had a single garage door closing from the top, the way modern doors do. But the garage was so old that it could not have been constructed that way. Then when I was excavating the accumulation of family photographs looking for images for the book's cover, I found a picture that included the double doors of the garage. I had been conflating my mother's story with other remembered images of single garage doors closing from the top and resting against a car's bumper.

Part of the problem is that I was not remembering the event itself, but rather my mother's telling of the story. I had no images except the ones created in my head by the words my mother used. Having no first-hand visual memories of your own could obviously lead to gross inaccuracies.

Involuntary memories, on the other hand, are not distorted by the ego or confabulation. They just pop up; there's no time for them to be distorted. You're involved in some mindless repetitive task like washing windows or folding clothes, and you flash on a memory of your date for the high school prom. You haven't thought of this person in years, but because the memory is involuntary (you weren't trying to recall this person, you were just working) it will likely be accurate.

So a memory that pops into your head unbidden is pretty sure to be genuine. But if you consciously strive to recall an event, you should take care to assure accuracy.

One of the ways of accomplishing that is to interview other participants in the event.

Journal/Notes

Journal/Notes

Journal/Notes

Journal/ Notes

Chapter 6
Interviewing: Memory Extraction

A couple of reasons for interviewing someone are to get information for your own memoir or to get information if you're writing someone else's. Either way, there are a few common-sense rules for interviewing someone for the purpose of gathering information. (The other type of interview is for the personality profile for magazines, but that's a different animal.)

The 3 Ps
You must be...

Prompt. People are busy and they're giving you their time. Don't make them wait.

Professional. Even though you're probably not getting paid, at least be organized enough to appear professional; this will help to inspire confidence in your interviewee.

Polite. It'll help them like you, and as a result, you'll learn more.

Ask open ended questions. That means questions that require answers beyond "yes" or "no." Some people are shy and insecure and have never been interviewed, so if they see an opportunity not to talk they'll take it. For instance:

"Was life difficult on the farm when you were young?" Bad form here. Three possible answers: yes, no, kinda. Sure they might elaborate without your asking, but there are no guarantees.

"How difficult was life on a farm when you were little?" Better, but no Pulitzer. They have to give you a more fleshed out answer, but the question is leading. If you use the word difficult in the question, your interviewee will think you want to write about hard times, so they'll tend to accommodate you.

"What was your typical day on the farm?" Best example. No leading, no agenda, you just want to know what things were like.

Help your interviewee to feel safe by making your interview a conversation and not an interrogation. In fact, depending on the person you're talking to, you might not even want to call it an interview. Call it a chat with an agenda. Some people have never been interviewed in their lives, so they might be a little nervous, or at least very aware of the fact that you're writing down what they say.

Be interested, don't just act interested. You probably are indeed attentive to what the interviewee is saying, but you must be sure to communicate the fact. Provide feedback, those nods and vocalizations ("Really? How interesting.") that evidence your attention. Writer Henry Walshak interviews people for his histories of colleges and other institutions. He refers to this evidence of the interviewer's interest as "verbally leaning forward." Hank uses this technique in telephone interviews, but it works face-to-face as well.

That brings up another point people always ask me about. "Which should I use," they ask, "a notebook or a tape recorder?" The answer is yes, use both, after you have asked permission. In some cases, you're recording what amounts to an oral history, so you want to get it all and get it right. So yes, use a voice recorder.

Pencils break, pens dry up, batteries die. If you have the budget, take a backup for everything. Extra pens, notebooks, batteries, tapes, even an extra recorder are in order. I had two micro-cassette recorders for taking notes, one for home and one that I kept in the car. They both died on the same day. I still believe it was a suicide pact.

Please don't obsess about the recorder. If you do, so will your interviewee. If you're sitting across from them at a table, don't plop the recorder down between the two of you. It will lay there like a sick cat on the vet's examination table, and your interviewee won't be able to resist looking at it. Move it off to the side and continue the conversation, making eye contact and directing the focus to the conversation and not to the technology. When your friend isn't looking, glance at the recorder to check how much tape is left and that the machine is still running.

Be certain of the ins and outs of using the recorder. The record button, the play button, fast forward, rewind, etc. Get a recorder with some sort of counter or timer. During the conversation, you'll use the notebook to jot down a word or phrase that you know you'll want to refer to later. Beside the notation, you'll write the counter/ timer reading. Later you can go directly to the place on the recording that holds the relevant information, and you won't need to search through the whole interview.

That being said, I still recommend reviewing the entire recording at some point. You might have missed something valuable.

Have a plan, a list of questions to ask and areas to cover. Just remember that it's a guide, not a script. If your friend takes off on a tangent only marginally related to the topic at hand, decide how interesting it is. You might be pleasantly surprised. Use your tact and judgment.

You might need to address some delicate areas in your subject's life. Ask these touchy questions at the end, after you have all the other information you need. These are the questions about skeletons in the closets: love affairs, embezzlement, horse thievery, jail terms. If you ask these questions first, your friend might get upset and end the interview and you'll have nothing. Start with softballs, then make the questions edgier if you need to.

Warm-up Questions: Wide-Angle or Close-up?

The wide-angle or close-up distinction is similar to the era-episode-event technique of memory recall in that you are asking questions conforming to either a broad or narrow coverage of a topic. And the decision on which technique to use is based on the personality of your interviewee.

Wide-angle questions are broad in scope.

Tell me about World War II.

Such an opener should be directed to the person who has no trouble talking. This person has a well of stories, is always primed to tell them, and exemplifies the raconteur, the affable conversationalist. You can ask the more focused questions later in the interview.

Close-up questions are much more tightly focused.

What did they put you through in army training camp?

Questions like these are for the shy people or people who are not accustomed to being interviewed. Or even to being listened to very closely. You need to get them warmed up, draw them out.

After you've put them through this ordeal, don't forget the thank-you note.

Silence: Learn When to Pause

In the chapter on dialogue, I mentioned silences and how they practically never happen in good movie dialogue or in well-rendered distilled conversation. However, silence can be useful in an interview.

You might have noticed a technique used by reporters in their standup interviews. You see a close-up of the person being interviewed and the reporter's hand holding the microphone in their face. The person finishes the sentence, but the savvy reporter, sensing something else might be coming, remains silent and continues to hold the microphone in front of the interviewee. The poor civilian, not being wise to this trick, assumes more is expected of him, so he says something off the cuff. He blurts. And it's probably more interesting and revealing than what he has already said. Watch for it on your local news. If the scene doesn't cut right after the speaker finishes a sentence, you know something more is coming.

You can use this technique in a *limited* fashion in your interviews. Many a novice interviewer has cut off a potentially fascinating answer because the person paused, and the interviewer rushed ahead to the next question on the list. As a culture, we Americans get antsy during conversational silences, and so we rush to fill the vacuum. Don't be so quick to fill the silence. Pause once in a while to see if there is more to come. Don't do this every time, or the interviewee will think you're dull-witted. Use your common sense, your listening ability, and the interviewee's nonverbal cues. If you pay attention, you can often tell whether or not someone has more to say.

Journal/Notes

Journal/ Notes

Journal/ Notes

Journal/Notes

Chapter 7
Interlude:
A Cautionary Tale about Writing

Writing illuminates. And sometimes it throws light into dark corners.

Memoir writing means writing about memories. In fact, the words memoir and memory both come from the same Latin root, *memoria*. The usual methods of bobbing for memories are such triggers as sights, sounds, smells, old photographs, period music... the list goes on. But sometimes the very act of writing about the present can dredge up events from the past that we might prefer to leave hidden.

For instance:

Late afternoon on a sunny August day. I was sitting in rush hour traffic on a four-lane bridge behind a red convertible, never mind what make, I can't tell them apart. (Pulling fifty from the uphill side, and still, the only models I recognize are Volkswagen Beetles and whatever I happen to be driving that year.) A panel truck was stopped in front of the convertible. The car's top was down and I could see the driver fussing with business-type papers next to him on the passenger seat, oblivious to the rest of the world. Slowly I realized that parallax and perspective were warping: his car was getting larger.

He was still shuffling his papers, not realizing that his car was drifting slowly backwards, toward me. I had no idea what gear he was in, and he certainly didn't. I laid on my horn for a good five seconds — he never heard it — before his bumper tapped mine. Obviously startled, he glared at me in his rearview mirror. By then the truck in front of him had moved ahead, so Mr. Convertible lurched ahead, too. Employing a traditional hand signal, he told me that he was number one, he just used the more aggressive finger.

As we crossed the bridge, he purposely slowed down in front of me and fired dirty looks at me in his rearview mirror. Stopping at a red light at the other end of the bridge, he shot out of his car and strode toward me. Late forties. Typical business uniform of the day: blue blazer, gray slacks, blue-and-white striped shirt. Salt-and-pepper hair sculpted and blow-dried. As he stomped toward me, he exhaled the expected platitudes. "What the hell? What's your problem, buddy?!" And so on. He got to my window and as he inhaled for another salvo, and I said firmly, gently, the way you tell a nine-year-old he's standing on your foot, "You drifted back into me."

Without moving, the man deflated.

He had been convinced that I had grown impatient sitting behind him and had decided to blow my horn at him and use my intimidating '92 Skylark to goose him into gear. I could tell that his indignation had so crowded his head that it left no room for the possibility that he was the one at fault. He looked at me, then at his car. That gave me enough time to repeat, "You drifted back into

90

me."

It was like looking into his head. One instant he was the aggrieved victim, then he morphed into the typical airheaded motorist that he had believed me to be a nanosecond before. I could see the realization wash over him that it was possible — indeed probable — that multitasking was not his strong suit, that he had been more interested in paying attention to two ounces of paper than to two thousand pounds of car. His final words to me were stated with the same quavering conviction as that same nine-year-old, this time professing ignorance as to who ate the pie Mom made for company: "I did not." He hurried back to his car, got in, and never looked at me in his rearview again.

Why was I easy on him? you're asking. I was the aggrieved party. Had I followed standard, modern procedure for the situation, I would have loosed a blast of verbal napalm that would reduce Mr. Convertible to a pillar of ash. But I didn't — most likely because of a childhood memory that was awakened, groggy and bleary-eyed, by my writing about the here and now.

Writing illuminates.

Many of us dislike accepting responsibility. Including me. I must have been nine when this happened, so I was likely in the third grade. We went home for lunch in those years, and I was with a crowd of kids headed for an intersection and a student crossing guard. You remember them: they got to wear a white web belt and wave a cardboard stop sign and tell on you if you screwed up. Report kids, we called them.

I was jostling and pushing and generally skylarking along with the others as we crossed the street. I vaguely noted bumping a kid who was not participating in the jostling; rather, he was simply trying to cross the street and go home and have his lunch. As I got to the other side, the report kid stopped me. "You knocked that kid's glasses off," he said, "and they broke."

91

I responded immediately, never checking to see if I had indeed knocked someone's glasses off, never even stopping to think, just sliding effortlessly into an actor's studio expression of innocence carried off with throwaway aplomb. "I didn't break anyone's glasses."

Maybe I did, maybe I didn't. I never found out. I was too busy convincing the report kid of my "innocence." Then I did something that I repressed for years.

Fifteen feet away was the corner of a side street formed by a six-foot high wall. Getting around that corner would take me out of sight of the report kid and, three blocks farther, to the safety of home, where lunch was waiting. But I had to get there easily. Convincingly. With an unequivocal display of innocence.

So I skipped.

No kid skips today. Hell, no self-respecting kid skipped *then*. But I did. I skipped to and around that corner like a sissy. Like a coward. Like the guy in the convertible who couldn't cop to being wrong. I was no better than he was. Maybe that's why I was so easy on him: he was me, a generation or so later. Did the frames of the kid's glasses merely crack and his mother could tape them together and he could still wear them? Or did a lens shatter and he needed them to actually see and his parents couldn't afford to replace them? It was a small town, and a lot of parents knew whose kids were whose. I never heard anything more about it, so logic tells me the former scenario was probably the case.

But the fact remains, I skipped.

Today, Mr. Convertible's excuse for not admitting wrongdoing is the fear of a lawsuit. What was my excuse when I was nine?

I would have preferred that the memory had remained hidden away in the shadows of my subconscious because obviously I don't like what I did. Writing about one memory can stir up a nest of others.

Beware: writing illuminates.

Chapter 8
Choose Your Rules:
Writing about your life the common-sense way

Writing is the best way to tell future generations who we were and what we did. But many of us, if presented with the choice between committing words to a page and performing a do-it-yourself root canal, would be surfing the web, looking to order Novocaine in bulk. Why? Because we're afraid.

We're afraid that we're going to miss a rule. That one of those axioms that were ground into us in "grammar school" (a misnomer, fortunately; imagine an entire school devoted solely to grammar) will slip into our writing, and we will forever be judged by a split infinitive (I'll tell you what that is) or a preposition dangling off the end of a sentence like a stray bag of grass clippings about to fall off the back of the yard boy's pickup. (We must also be on the watch for overly long sentences, for sentence fragments, and for similes stretched to the breaking

point, of which the foregoing construction is an example.)
(And we must guard against using too many parentheses.)

Writing can be fun, and the reading of it enjoyable. Yet while enjoying the process of writing, we ought to write with an awareness of two things: there are indeed rules of grammar and usage, and we will be judged if we flaunt them.

But how seriously do we need to take the rules? The answer: fairly seriously, but not fanatically.

What follows are not all the rules, certainly; this is not a grammar book. But during my twenty-five years of teaching, the following nits have ossified into the major bones of contention. Because writing about your life should be in your own informal voice, some of these rules can be bent, even ignored. Some, not all. I've clearly indicated which ones are which.

Avoid beginning a sentence with a conjunction

And who says so? Granted, this does not conform to a strictly formal style of writing. But when you want your prose to be approachable and casual and sound more like conversation, it's the way to go. Treat this advice as you would sweets during the holidays: don't overdo it.

Not ending a sentence with a preposition is a proposition I don't subscribe to. That's one of Robert Lowth's gems. Lowth was an 18th century clergyman and grammarian. Ironically, there were many experts on religion back then and precious few on English. But Lowth was undeterred; in 1762, he published *A Short Introduction to English Grammar*. Would that he had not. Not so much for what he said, but for what he inspired: yet more books on grammar. He devised many of the rules that we as children were forced to learn. At least he wrote the book in English; earlier publications about English grammar were written in Latin. Lowth's reported position on prepositions was that ending a sentence with one was inelegant.

Be careful in ignoring this rule, because everybody knows it. That is to say, they know you're not *supposed* to end a sentence with a preposition, but they probably couldn't tell you why. They "know" it's wrong, and in the knowing comes the judging. The reader might tend to discount your statement because it isn't expressed according to the rules.

So post-position your prepositions with care, but for me, this is an issue up about which I can't get worked.

Avoid splitting an infinitive. Lowth and others said you shouldn't split an infinitive because it wasn't done in Latin. Well, here's a bulletin for you: it *couldn't* be done in Latin. In English, an infinitive (the prime form of a verb) is usually considered to be made up of two words, "to" and the verb itself. To love. To laugh. To learn. In Latin, the infinitive form is only one word. *Amare. Ridere. Discere.* You couldn't split the infinitive without fracturing the word itself.

Now don't go running off splitting infinitives willy nilly. An infinitive is split by inserting an adverb (which modifies, or limits, the verb). Interring the adverb in the middle of the infinitive can place the emphasis on the verb instead of on the modifier (the adverb) where you probably want it. Compare:

> to completely comprehend (emphasis on the verb)
> to comprehend completely (emphasis on the ad verb)

> to truly love   (emphasis on the verb)
> to love truly   (emphasis on the adverb)

All right, you say, but what about the captain of the starship Enterprise intoning, "*to boldly go* where no one has gone before"? Is the adverb buried? Yes. Is the

96

emphasis misplaced? Yes, but only in writing. In speaking, we can emphasize the words and syllables necessary to produce the desired effect. Next time, listen to the way William Shatner or Patrick Stewart interprets that line. "To BOLDly GO where NO one has GONE beFORE." Those words were written by a script writer, and these writers create dialogue for the ear, not the eye. Those words were written to be said, not read.

Historical bonus: All writing was originally intended to be spoken aloud. Reading silently to oneself was unheard of (sorry) until somewhere around the beginning of the second millennium.

May you split an infinitive? Of course you may. The true tests of the construction are two: Is it clear? Does it flow?

Only

Speaking of emphasis, that leads us to another often misplaced element of a sentence: the modifier "only". Consider this statement: I like eating oatmeal with raisins. Where does "only" belong? Most of us would say, "I only like eating oatmeal with raisins." Taken in a restricted sense (on the page), it sounds as thought the only emotion we're dealing with is "liking." I only *like* eating oatmeal with raisins. No loving, no hating, simply liking. But we're actually saying, "I like eating oatmeal only *when it contains raisins*." In the first example, if we moved "only" any farther from the intended modifiee, it would practically be in another sentence. "Only" should come just before or very close to the word to be modified.

May vs. might.

Here's another case of intonation supporting meaning. In the strictest senses of these words, "may" connotes permission and "might" connotes possibility. However, "may" is often used for possibility in casual speech. But in order to be completely understood, the

97

word needs oral and sometimes visual support. "I may go to the concert." Strict sense: I am allowed to go to the concert. If we want that sentence to connote possibility, we need to see hands waffling back and forth and to hear a tentative, half-whiny inflection in the voice. Absent context, we are left with the possibility of confused meanings.

Dangling modifying phrases

Walking along the sidewalk, a truck backfired and scared John. The truck was probably not walking along the sidewalk; rather, John was. Try this: "A backfiring truck frightened John as he walked along the sidewalk."

Active voice vs. passive voice

Passive voice has received a lot of negative press recently, much of it unfair. Mostly you'll hear that it's a weak way of saying something. Sometimes it is, but not always.

First, an example: John threw the ball. This sentence is written in the active voice because the subject of the sentence, John, is acting on the object, the ball.

Another example: The ball was thrown by John. This is passive voice in that subject is the ball, and it is being acted upon by John, the object. There's nothing inherently wrong with either voice as far as meaning is concerned. Both describe a ball flying through the air after being propelled by John. But using the passive voice in this instance serves no purpose. It just slows down the reader. Let's view the sentence slowly. First we see a ball, then we learn it has been thrown, and not until the very end of the sentence are we allowed to see who threw it.

A choice must be made by the writer: where does the emphasis belong? Answer (you're not going to like this): it depends.

It depends on two factors: how you can best allow the reader to visualize the action and whose story you're telling.

Visualization: Let's say you're describing the effects of a storm on someone's home. *The wind blew down the house.* Now, most times, writers are trying to paint pictures in their readers' minds. How do we visualize the wind? By its effects. We cannot see the actual wind, only the objects being blown around by it: newspapers, tree branches, cows. So if you're appealing to the reader's visual sense, you're better off making the subject something that can be seen. Try this: *the house was blown down by the wind.* Your reader can easily visualize the house, and besides, let's face it, the house itself is passive.

Whose story: Let's say someone carries someone else up some steps, perhaps because of illness, age, or injury. If you're telling the story about the carrier, use the active voice. *Mary carried Grandpa up the steps.* But if the reader's focus should be on the person being carried, use the passive voice. *Grandpa was carried up the steps by Mary.*

There are always alternate ways to describe an event. Maybe you want to show passivity, but you don't want to de-emphasize either person's role in the sentence. *Grandpa was so frail that Mary had to carry him up the steps.*

Agreement of a pronoun with a preceding noun of ambiguous gender

This sounds like a mind-bender, but stay with me. Example: One of the students left the classroom without taking his or her book. "His or her" sounds awkward, but is necessary if we are to avoid the sexist tradition of assuming that every ambiguous noun representing a person is masculine. Before the 70s enlightenment, one would have written: One of the students left the classroom without taking his book. Unless the memory lapse took place in an all-boys school, it's regarded as sexist to presume the student was male. But is there any other solution except for the one put forth at the beginning of the paragraph? A student left the classroom and he or she forgot his or her book. Pretty cumbersome.

How do we streamline our writing when we must contend with the issue of agreement? English does not have a one-size-fits-all pronoun to cover this situation. Or does it? A few brave souls now advocate the plural pronoun "they," even though it is referring to a singular noun. A student left the classroom and forgot their book. It doesn't scan grammatically, but it's certainly shorter. (FYI, I can't bring myself to embrace this solution.) Creative alternatives have surfaced: "s/he," for instance. Some consider it loathsome. I first saw it used in an essay by writer Harlan Ellison, and I think it's nicely streamlined. It just happens to be unpronounceable.

Alright vs. all right

Webster's second edition © 1970, states that "alright" is used often, but is substandard. The Concise Oxford English Dictionary, © 1999, says about the same thing. The Harbrace College Handbook, © 1986, says that "alright" is not yet considered an alternative for "all right." Times change. In a recent French film *Sous le Sable (Under the Sand)*, the subtitles use "alright" freely, as have many other writers of late. It has not achieved unconditional acceptance, but it's a matter only of time. It might be similar to what has happened to formerly hyphenated words. As recently as the 1940s we had "to-day" and "to-night." Then the hyphen gradually disappeared.

Comprise

The word has a nice ring to it, doesn't it? It makes the writer seem literate and discerning. Unfortunately, it's misused more than half the time. There are words that should never bump into one another, and two of them are "comprise" and "of". A school is not comprised of students, teachers, and chalk dust. Rather, it is composed or made up of them. Use "comprise" as you would use "embrace" or "contain". A school "comprises" students, teachers, etc.

100

Flammable

In writing about your life, I hope you won't have much use for the word "flammable", but if you do, here's the scoop. It's one of the few words that have changed for a good reason: safety. The original form of the word was "inflammable", meaning able to inflame or catch fire. The in part was never a negating prefix *a la* "inoperable" or "inclement". But it was perceived as such. There are no statistics I know of that tally how many drivers saw "inflammable" painted on a tanker truck and thought they could plow into it without being incinerated. Other tankers carrying such non-incendiary cargo as water or milk tried using "non-inflammable"; you can imagine the confusion. Eventually, the usage switched to "flammable" and "non-flammable". Then they replaced "flammable" with a placard sporting a *picture* of fire. Now the illiterati, too, are safe.

Hopefully

"Hopefully", depending on its placement, has gotten a bad rap as a dangling adverb with nothing in particular to modify. *"Will you go out with me?" he said hopefully.* No problem here; the man is asking his question in a hopeful manner. *Hopefully, it will be a nice day.* "Horrors!" cry the grammarians. "The day can not be nice in a hopeful manner." *Sadly*, this outcry ignores perfectly understandable sentences such as this one. Such an adverb, it can be argued, modifies the tone or impact of the entire sentence rather than only the verb. *Fortunately*, we need not worry overmuch about this rule. *Conceivably*, there will come the day when no one worries about it. Alright, I'll stop.

Nouns used as adjectives

This insidious problem is creeping into everyday business communication, and it won't be long before it's popping up everywhere, including memoirs. The prob-

101

lem is bad because it causes confusion. I would be guilty of this if I gave this book the title *Memoir Writing Instruction Manual*. All four of these words are nouns ("writing" is a gerund, a noun form of a verb). The title would be understandable ... eventually, but not immediately. It's perfectly fine to use one noun as an adjective (I did it in the first sentence of this section with the phrase "business communication"), but don't use a whole string of them.

Nouns used as verbs then changed to adjectives ... or something
I heard a radio commercial a few years ago at Christmastime announcing that Santa would hand out free toys to children at a local store. The announcer actually said: Children under ten will be gifted.

Nouns used as verbs
Overheard in a bar: "Beer me!" Enough said.

You cannot completely forget the rules, even in the most casual writing, because the words must flow smoothly, uninterrupted. You want the reader to be so involved in your story that they forget they're reading. Misspelled words, poor grammar, and incorrect usage provide hiccups in the flow of words and images. The reader comes to an error, and suddenly those pictures you were painting in their mind vanish, replaced by words on a page. And incorrect ones at that.

Most mistakes in writing are made, I believe, in the haste to be done with a distasteful task. But if you make it fun and play with the rules and don't take it too seriously, writing can be as enjoyable as reading.

Above all, don't be afraid. Writing isn't a root canal.

Chapter 9
The Act of Writing

Location, location, location

Where is the best place to write? Only you can answer that question.

Award winning news stories have been written in noisy, bustling offices. Great novels have been written at kitchen tables. It's about concentration.

I once read of a professional writer who worked at home. He was a family man with a loving wife and children. While he was devoted to his family, he also needed his time to work. So he made a sign and hung it on the outside of his office door. It said simply:

"Not now."

(This story is also told of Sid Caesar and the sign he would hang on his office door while he was working on sketches for his 50s classic, "Your Show of Shows.")

Many writers, needing to escape the home environment, enjoy writing in coffee shops. (Maybe we should name our writing muse Juana Valdez.) I know a minister who writes his sermons in the café of a Border's Bookstore. I know this because that's where I write, too. Speculative fiction writer-novelist-essayist Harlan Ellison took writing in public a step or two further, having written many stories while sitting at his typewriter in book store windows. For all these writers, it's a matter of tuning out the external surroundings and tuning in to the words-on-the-page part of the process.

For me, writing in the café is a way of getting away from the distractions of home … and replacing them with other distractions. But at least the distractions at the café are ones that I need not trouble myself with. Out of coffee? Someone makes me a fresh cup. Floor dirty? Someone sweeps it. Plants thirsty? A young lady from the plant service comes in and waters them.

Words of warning: If you spend time at the café and become a regular, there is the danger that you'll make friends there. Those friends will want to be friendly when they see you and might reason that you're only tapping a keyboard and will be open to conversation. If you want to be undisturbed, try the library or stay home. The other danger of both the library and the book store is the siren call of all those books. Get back to work, and resist the urge to browse.

Writers groups

Writers groups can be wonderful support for an otherwise solitary pursuit. Having said that, I don't advise talking about your writing project too soon. Many writers believe that talking about a project can sap the energy needed for writing it. Maybe the creative effort you expend describing the potential of the project comes from the same place as the creative effort of writing. Then again, maybe it's nothing other than the fact that getting together for a writers group meeting is just one of the multitude of excuses we come up with for not writing. And these excuses are legion:

I should really tidy up this desk.

Or…

The cat is napping with his/her head resting on the keyboard.

Or…

Boy, those Venetian blinds sure are dusty.

Or…

Boy, I really need some Venetian blinds.

(If writers were as creative with their writing as they are with coming up with excuses for not writing, they'd all be neck-deep in Pulitzers.)

Reasons abound for talking about writing, even about a specific project. Usually those reasons are technique- or business-related. What voice and POV should I use? How do I get a publisher? Should I ask open ended or tightly focused questions in an interview? Valid questions, all. But at the beginning stages, all your energy should be directed toward the writing. Why talk about your project when you could be accomplishing it? Talk about your project after you have a first draft or are at least far enough along to have something to report.

However, if you're stuck or need some encouragement, talking with other writers is the way to go. In this solitary confinement that is writing, you need to talk to someone besides yourself. That other someone might have some personal insights that fit your situation. If not, you're still away from the keyboard and can accumulate some new impressions.

So… for specific advice on a project, wait until you're farther along in that project. For encouragement, get to a meeting, just keep mum about your project.

In short, don't talk about what you plan to write, talk about what you've written.

Subconscious writing

The implementation part of the process is more than simply writing down what surfaced from the inspiration phase. Inspiration and implementation are closely allied, even inseparable. Just as you write things down during inspiration, so are you inspired during the actual setting down of words.

Allow your subconscious to help out during the writing part of the process. It works. In fact, you probably have had experience with the phenomenon already. Have you ever gone to bed with a problem? Let me rephrase that: have you ever gone to bed with a problem weighing on your mind? Maybe it's a dilemma for which you're seeking a solution or a minor problem you're trying to resolve. You go to sleep, and then you wake up in the morning with the answer filling your head like the morning sun flooding your bedroom. Your subconscious has been working all night to untie the knots, without any conscious effort on your part.

It might have happened with a trick of memory. You run into someone whose name escapes you. You know the name — you *know* you know the name — but it eludes you, like a cat in a big house. Then you go about your business and, later, unbidden, the name springs to mind. You weren't even thinking about the person, not consciously, at least. Your subconscious did it for you, working in the shadows, and when it had the name, it nudged it into the light where you could see it. There was indeed effort, just not the conscious variety.

Ideas and phrases tend to surface while doing brainless tasks, or at least things that allow the mind to wander. During long car trips on open stretches of highway, your mind takes the occasional detour. A small tape recorder can store all the gems, rough and otherwise. Washing dishes is another activity requiring minimal attention. If you don't have a dishwasher already, don't buy one.

Judgment day

Even though you might be writing your stories solely for your family, you still want them to believe you. Because your ideas will be judged in part by the quality of their expression, you need to be careful about some of the technical aspects of this craft. (For more details, see the "Choose Your Rules" chapter.) Many people write only when they need to send a business e-mail and avoid any other kind of writing. These benighted souls live in a world in which capitalization is elitist, punctuation is optional, and Spell-check might as well be the name of the U.N. ambassador from Belarus. Memoir writers must be better than that. Of course, worrying about quality leads to anxiety about writing, and anxiety just sets up roadblocks to creativity.

This anxiety sets you up for failure, or at the very least, more difficulty than is necessary. Some sad folks, when they absolutely must write something, produce more flop sweat than a skinhead comedian on open mike night at the Apollo. Fingers on the keyboard, they attempt Shakespeare right out of the gate. They envision perfect, pristine paragraphs springing full-blown like Athena from Zeus's forehead. Even Will himself couldn't pull that off. Shakespeare made notes, wrote lists, and scribbled semi-legible ideas on scraps of foolscap. All that iambic pentameter? He put that in later.

It's easier to write something if you start out not treating it as something you have to compose. Write whatever is in your head, without editing on the fly. You can't fix what isn't written yet, but that's what many people try to do. Once you have words on a page, you can tinker with them. Delete. Add. Rearrange. Alas, maybe even start over.

Be bold and write the way Shakespeare did: daydream, make lists, jot notes and randomly occurring phrases. Take the pressure off. Remember, the early stages of the process don't involve writing at all, only thinking.

You're sitting in your chair, looking out the window (if you have one), watching the birds … and thinking. Someone walks by and sees you and says, "What're you doing?"

Still gazing at the birds, you reply, "Writing."

And you are.

Getting the Ideas

After you've mentally catalogued all the species of birds visible from your window, you might actually want to write something. But how to start. For establishing momentum, nothing beats freewriting. Freewriting has two meanings: *free* as in free to write without worries about style, and *free* as in no one else will see it, so you can write anything that comes into your head.

You start with a single topic, then write for five or ten minutes straight. You keep writing. If you can't think of anything to write, write that. Or rewrite your previous sentence. That means not stopping to read what you've written, not stopping to revise or reword; in short, not stopping. There is no pressure to spell correctly, use punctuation or capitalization, even to make sense.

Also called direct writing, freewriting accomplishes three things: gets you warmed up, establishes some forward momentum, and generates ideas. You won't use everything you come up with. Some of it will be nonsensical or banal or inane.

I gave this assignment to my students, with an added twist. They were seated at desktop computers with separate monitors. I had them turn off their monitors so they couldn't evaluate what they wrote. I advise that for you as well. If you use a laptop, place a piece of paper over the screen. If you're accustomed to looking at the screen as you write, try to adapt.

No one else should see what you write using this technique. This is just for you. Besides, this exercise has been known to dredge up some surprising results. Could

109

be memories, could be attitudes. You might even be disturbed by what comes out. That's another reason to keep the results of freewriting to yourself.

Let Your Writing Voice Be Heard

700 years ago the word "nice" meant "foolish." 700 years from now, it might mean that again. That brings up the question of language and meaning.

Write your stories in your own voice, using current expressions and terminology, even though your stories might be read many years in the future. The language in Shakespeare's plays is sometimes a bit difficult for modern audiences to decipher unless they happen to be scholars or aficionados. Remember, though, that Shakespeare wrote for his contemporaries, not for audiences 400 years in the future. But in your writing, you must walk a fine line.

Write in current common language, but at the same time, temper the tendency to use modern slang that might not last beyond the end of the week. Slang doesn't last as long as it used to because, with the advent of the Internet, it gets worn out from overuse much more quickly.

Your goal is to be understood in the future, and slang is so here-and-now that the odds are against your meaning getting through. There is of course always the possibility that a slang term will catch on and become a part of the vocabulary, e.g., *swell* and *cool*, but you have no way of knowing. Some compilers of books about slang say that it evolves rapidly. That's a nice way of saying that it generally tends to have a short shelf life. Some slang endures while some disappears. Beware: the use of slang will pigeon-hole you. You will be judged by the slang-cant-patois-argot that you use. If you use computer slang, you're a nerd. If you use gangsta rap slang, you're a gang banger. If you use sports slang, you're a political pundit.

Jargon is out because it is so exclusionary. Jargon comprises terms that are specific to a discipline and that outsiders are not meant to understand. It didn't start out being exclusionary, that's simply a fact of language life. Lawyers have their subpoenas duces tecum and codicils and res gestae. Computer techs have their gigabytes, megapixels, and RAMs. Doctors have their alphabet soup of ECGs, NSAIDs, and SOBs (that means "short of breath" in case you were wondering).

Expressions, however, are fine. They can serve as a barometer of the times, and giving future readers a feel for the zeitgeist is a fine side effect of your narrative. Imagine how enlightening a letter from an ancestor would be, complete with contemporary (for them) expressions. Granted, you might miss some nuances of meaning within expressions such as:

A man of my kidney

A pig in a poke

Three sheets to the wind (We know what the expression signifies, but many of us don't know what it *means*.)

Here's an expression-vs.-book metaphor for you. Think of your favorite current nonfiction book that has been recently published. Now think of that same book 50 years from today. It will be dated, but still informative. It will be a snapshot of the world at that time. *The Trouble with Advertising*, by John O'Toole, is still in print as this writing. It is learned, informative, well-crafted, all those good things. What it is not is current; the hard-cover edition came out in 1982. It is now a wonderful book on advertising history; O'Toole just didn't intend it to be that.

The best voice in which to write is obviously your own. And that includes favorite figurative expressions. But will future audiences understand you? Yes, if your expressions aren't too slangy and *au courant*. (Avoid foreign terms as well; they're so *déclassé*.) But if you wish to use colorful expressions, use ones that are easily figured out. Such as:

So 10 minutes ago.

111

What's up with that?

Whatever!

(Substitute the current expressions that are in vogue when you're reading this.)

The Issue of Time

Most people set aside time to write, maybe an hour a day or a couple of hours a week. Try setting a goal: say a page a day. Or set a time limit: finish the project by Thanksgiving.

I can hear you now: I'd love to write, I just don't have the time.

Time issues are directly proportional to your desire to write. There's wanting to write and then there's needing to write. If you need to write, you'll find the time. You'll steal time from other things you should be accomplishing. You won't be able *not* to write.

However, if you're a normal person who simply wants to set down your stories on paper, you'll have more difficulty finding time to write. That's because you have your priorities in order. You know that, instead of writing, you need to walk the dog and shop for food and do your laundry, and so you tend to these tasks.

Procrastination in the writing of life stories is dangerous in that crucial details can be lost over time. People's memories fade or become influenced by outside factors until they're no longer reliable. And if you want to interview others for their memories, don't put it off. People leave this world every day, and they take the answers to the unasked questions with them.

Journal/ Notes

Journal/ Notes

Journal/ Notes

Journal/ Notes

Chapter 10
The Butterfly Effect
Or "It doesn't cost anything to pay attention."

Have you heard of the butterfly effect? It derives from chaos theory, which states that minuscule causes can lead to monumental effects. It led Edward Lorenz, a meteorologist and researcher, to give a presentation that asked the question, "Can the Flap of a Butterfly's Wings in Brazil Set Off a Tornado in Texas?"

I believe the answer is yes, at least symbolically.

In the late seventies, after graduating from art school with a degree in photography, I worked for a photo lab for little money, so little that I couldn't afford to go away for vacation. My first apartment was in a house with a decent back yard, and that's where I decided to spend the sunny summer days of my week off. The property was surrounded by trees out of which came the twittering of birds, so I figured that counted as communing with nature.

I sat in a lawn chair (because I didn't have a chaise), shirt off, reading and soaking up the sun. The second day of that week, I was sunning and reading when I felt a fluttering on my left shoulder. I turned and pulled my head back as far as I could in order to focus, and I saw a monarch butterfly.

The butterfly simply rested there on my shoulder, wings wafting gently in the light breeze. Ordinarily, I don't like anyone reading over my shoulder, but I was willing to make an exception in this unusual circumstance. I didn't see any reason to brush it away since butterflies aren't poisonous and I had never heard of one sinking its talons into its prey and flying off with it to feast. So we both sunned ourselves. After a while, it fluttered away. "How interesting," I thought. "Nature is communing with me."

The next day was sunny, so I returned to my post in the back yard. Only a few moments after sitting down, I felt a familiar flutter on my shoulder. The same butterfly was back, resting on the same shoulder. So we spent some more time together.

It happened yet again the next day.

Three days in a row. Same back yard, same butterfly, same shoulder.

This is the only story in the book that has no ending, because, to this day, I'm not completely certain what I was being told. If it was a sign, it was a subtle one, because nothing life-altering happened to me around that time. Later I took it as a sign to pay attention to the little things, because they can lead to bigger ones.

I'm still paying attention.

Noticing and recording the minute details of a life will result in a monumental accumulation of events. And it is from these events that grand stories grow.